# NATURE'S CHILDREN™

# KOALAS

*by Josh Gregory*

**Children's Press®**

An Imprint of Scholastic Inc.

Content Consultant
Dr. Stephen S. Ditchkoff
Professor of Wildlife Ecology and Management
Auburn University
Auburn, Alabama

Photographs ©: cover: Minden Pictures/Superstock, Inc.; 1: Craig
Dingle/Getty Images; 2-3 background: Hel080808/Dreamstime;
2 inset: Lydia/Dreamstime; 5 inset top: Tpgimages/Dreamstime;
5 inset bottom: Joel Sartore/National Geographic Creative; 7:
Stephanie Swartz/Dreamstime; 8: Lydia/Dreamstime; 11: Tpgimages/
Dreamstime; 12: markrhiggins/Thinkstock; 14, 15: ARCO/Mosebach
K/age fotostock; 16: NaturePL/Superstock, Inc.; 18, 19: Mark
Newman/Superstock, Inc.; 20, 21: woodstock/iStockphoto; 22, 23:
Marc Witte/Shutterstock, Inc.; 24: Gerard Lacz Images/Superstock,
Inc.; 27: D. Parer & E. Parer-Cook/Minden Pictures/Superstock, Inc.;
28, 29: Guillaume Souvant/AFP/Getty Images; 31: Robert Harding
World Imagery/Alamy Images; 32, 33: Craig Dingle/Getty Images;
34, 35: Travelmages/Shutterstock, Inc.; 36, 37: Jay Bray/Alamy
Images; 38, 39: Joel Sartore/National Geographic Creative; 40,
41: benjamint444/iStockphoto; 44-45 background: Hel080808/
Dreamstime; 46: Craig Dingle/Getty Images.

Map by Bob Italiano

Library of Congress Cataloging-in-Publication Data
Gregory, Josh, author.
 Koalas / by Josh Gregory.
  pages cm. — (Nature's children)
 Summary: "This book details the life and habits of koalas"— Provided
by publisher.
 Includes bibliographical references and index.
 ISBN 978-0-531-22720-6 (library binding) — ISBN 978-0-531-
22518-9 (pbk.)
 1. Koala—Juvenile literature. I. Title. II. Series: Nature's children (New
York, N.Y.)
 QL737.M384G76 2016
 599.2'5—dc23                    2015020023

Printed in China 62
SCHOLASTIC, CHILDREN'S PRESS, and associated logos are
trademarks and/or registered trademarks of Scholastic Inc.

1 2 3 4 5 6 7 8 9 10 R 25 24 23 22 21 20 19 18 17 16

# Koalas

| | |
|---:|:---|
| **Class** | Mammalia |
| **Order** | Diprotodontia |
| **Family** | Phascolarctidae |
| **Genus** | *Phascolarctos* |
| **Species** | *Phascolarctos cinereus* |
| **World distribution** | Eastern Australia |
| **Habitat** | Forests with a large number of eucalyptus trees |
| **Distinctive physical characteristics** | Roughly 27 to 32 inches (69 to 81 centimeters) tall; males weigh 21 to 30 pounds (9.5 to 13.6 kilograms); females are slightly smaller; fur ranges in color from gray to reddish brown; fur on underside is yellow or cream colored; large ears; small eyes; front paws have opposable thumbs as well as thumb-like opposable index fingers; sharp claws aid in climbing; rough pads on paws provide additional grip; strong arms and shoulders |
| **Habits** | Sleeps 18 to 20 hours per day on average, sometimes more; mostly nocturnal; solitary unless mating or raising young; makes a variety of roaring, grunting, bellowing, and screaming sounds to communicate; rarely leaves treetops; is an excellent climber |
| **Diet** | Eucalyptus leaves |

# Contents

# CHAPTER 1

# Sitting Still

It is a clear, quiet evening in a forest near the eastern coast of Australia. The sun has set, and the air is beginning to cool after a long summer day. A gentle breeze ruffles the leaves of the trees, but little else seems to be moving. High up in the crook of a nearby eucalyptus tree, there is a dark, round shape. Is it a clump of leaves? Some sort of bird's nest? Slowly, the shape begins to move. It's a koala!

As it wakes from a long nap, the koala stretches its neck and yawns with its mouth wide open. After a moment, it slowly reaches out to grab a nearby branch. Using a powerful arm, the koala pulls the branch down and begins plucking the green leaves with its mouth. After it is done eating, the koala is ready to take another nap. Once again, it settles down in between two sturdy branches and closes its eyes.

*A koala's fur helps it blend in with its treetop home.*

# A Closer Look

Koalas have a unique appearance that makes them immediately recognizable. Between a koala's tiny, round eyes lies a large, black nose. Huge fuzzy ears stick out from each side of the koala's head. The koala is covered almost completely in a heavy coat of fur. The fur ranges in color from dark gray to reddish brown on most of the koala's body. The animal's underside is a lighter cream or yellow color.

Koalas are not very large animals. Males are usually between 29.5 and 32 inches (75 and 81 centimeters) tall. They weigh between 20.9 and 29.8 pounds (9.5 and 13.5 kilograms). Females are slightly smaller. They are usually between 26.8 and 28.7 inches (68 and 73 cm) tall. Most weigh between 15.4 and 21.6 pounds (7 and 9.8 kg).

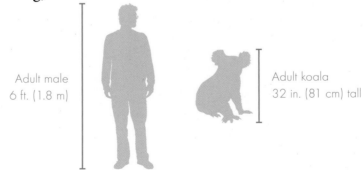

Adult male
6 ft. (1.8 m)

Adult koala
32 in. (81 cm) tall

*A koala's big nose and ears make it look very different from other medium-sized, furry animals.*

# Home Sweet Home

Some animals live in a wide range of habitats all around the world. However, koalas thrive in one very specific environment. They are found only in Australia, along the continent's eastern and southeastern coastlines, as well as on small islands nearby. They live in forests, but not just any trees will do. Koalas are found only in forests where certain types of eucalyptus trees are especially plentiful. These trees provide the koalas with both homes and food.

Many animals need some sort of shelter to make their homes. They might build nests or dig holes so they have somewhere to hide while sleeping. Koalas, on the other hand, are more than happy to simply sit down in a tree when it is time to rest. They especially like to wedge themselves into corners where sturdy branches stick out from a tree's trunk. The animals' stubby tails give them a comfortable pad to sit on.

*The crooks of branches are the most comfortable places for koalas to rest.*

# CHAPTER 2

# Looking for Leaves

Koalas have a very limited diet. They eat only leaves. Specifically, they eat only leaves that come from eucalyptus trees. Koalas are even picky about the types of eucalyptus. There are about 500 different species of eucalyptus tree. Koalas eat leaves from fewer than 50 of them. They especially like to nibble at the tips of the leaves. These are the softest and juiciest parts. Leaf tips also contain the most nutrients.

A koala spends around three hours each day eating. During this time, it might consume up to 2.5 pounds (1.1 kg) of leaves. Some of these leaves go into special pouches inside the koala's cheeks. This provides the koala with a quick snack if it gets hungry later on.

Koalas drink very little water. The leaves they eat are filled with moisture, and this gives them almost all the water they need. In fact, the name *koala* comes from an Aboriginal Australian word meaning "no drink."

*Koalas spend a lot of time every day eating leaves.*

# Dealing with Digestion

Eucalyptus leaves are not like the lettuce, spinach, and other leafy greens that you might eat in a salad. They are tough and extremely high in fiber. This means that a koala's favorite foods are very difficult to digest. However, a koala's digestive system is built specifically to deal with such tough foods. Special bacteria in a koala's large intestine help break down the leaves.

Koalas don't rely entirely on their intestines to deal with their leafy meals. Their first line of attack lies in their mouths. A koala's powerful teeth are perfectly shaped to grind eucalyptus leaves into fine particles. All that chewing puts a lot of wear and tear on the koala's teeth. As a koala grows older, its teeth wear down and become less effective. As a result, many elderly koalas have difficulty chewing up enough leaves to get the nutrients necessary to survive.

**FUN FACT!** Because they eat so many eucalyptus leaves, koalas are often described as smelling like eucalyptus cough drops.

*A koala's flat back teeth are perfect for grinding up leaves.*

# Reaching Great Heights

Because koalas spend so much time in the treetops, it makes sense that their bodies are built for climbing. They have very strong arms and shoulders. They also have sharp claws that can easily dig into the bark of trees. Each of a koala's front paws is equipped with an opposable thumb. This enables the koala to grip branches. A koala's index fingers are also opposable. This makes it look like it has two thumbs on each front paw. A koala's paws are equipped with rough pads that provide additional grip.

Koalas can climb up trees very quickly. They can also jump between branches that are not too far apart. When they need to move to a distant tree, however, they sometimes have to come down to the ground. When walking, they use all four limbs. The koala can also run at a fairly fast pace when necessary.

**FUN FACT!** Like humans, koalas have unique fingerprints. They are the only **mammals** other than primates to have them.

*Koalas can easily get a firm grip on branches using their opposable fingers.*

# A Koala's Senses

Koalas rely on a number of senses to help them navigate, find food, communicate, and avoid threats. For a koala, the most important sense of all is smell. A koala can sniff at leaves to tell the many different species of eucalyptus apart. This is especially important because some types of eucalyptus contain large amounts of toxins. These chemicals could make the koala sick if it ate them. The ability to tell these plants apart also allows the koala to choose a balanced diet of different eucalyptus varieties.

A koala's vision is its weakest sense. The animal's eyes are very small, and it cannot see well at all. On the other hand, with such large ears, koalas have terrific hearing abilities. The size and round shape of the ears make them perfect for picking up sound waves.

**FUN FACT!** Two toes on each of a koala's rear paws are joined together. The koala uses this double toe as a comb to clean its fur.

*Koalas often sniff leaves to help them decide whether or not they should eat them.*

# Survival Skills

Because koalas live out in the open, they must be able to deal with all kinds of weather. Their fur is coarse and thick. This helps keep a koala warm when it is cold. It also keeps the koala's skin from getting wet during a rainstorm. The water simply runs off the fur instead of soaking in. On hot days, koalas sleep with their bellies pointing toward the sun. When the weather is hot and sunny, lighter fur on the koala's underside reflects the sunlight. This helps keep the koala from overheating. Koalas also avoid the heat by finding trees with a lot of shade. They rest in the coolest parts of the tree, too, which are near the trunk.

Koalas face very few natural predators in the wild, especially once they are fully grown. However, Australian wild dogs called dingoes sometimes hunt koalas that come down from the treetops. On occasion, large owls attack koalas that are resting in trees.

*The light fur on a koala's underside helps it to stay cool on a hot, sunny day.*

# CHAPTER 3

# A Koala's Life

Koalas do not lead busy, active lives. They are happiest when they are left alone to sleep and eat leaves. Koalas spend an average of 18 to 20 hours every day napping or resting. Some days, they might sleep even more than that! The main reason for this is their diet. Eucalyptus leaves do not contain as many nutrients as other foods. In addition, digesting the leaves to absorb what nutrients they offer is a very slow process. Because of this, koalas do not have much energy to run around and be active. When koalas do decide to move about, it is almost always at night.

Koalas have very solitary lifestyles. Once they are fully grown, they don't usually spend time together. As a result, they are generally very quiet. However, they are capable of making a wide variety of noises when they do communicate. These sounds include roars, bellows, grunts, and screams.

*It takes a lot of energy for a koala to climb and leap from branch to branch.*

# Pairing Up

The one time adult koalas seek out each other's company is during **mating** season. Each year, from about August until February, males and females join together to produce young. Koalas advertise that they are ready to mate in several ways. One method that males use is to spread a special scent. The male koala has a bare spot on its chest where there is no fur. This spot is home to a scent **gland**. As the koala climbs around, it rubs the gland on trees, leaving its scent behind. When female koalas smell this scent, they know a potential mate is somewhere near.

Koalas also use noises to find mates. Females and males alike bellow loudly to attract each other. These sounds can offer important information about the koalas. Larger male koalas produce deeper sounds. Because females usually prefer larger mates, these low bellows can make one koala more attractive than its rivals.

*A male koala sticks its head into the air as it makes its mating calls.*

# Starting Out Small

After mating, male and female koalas go their separate ways. About five weeks later, the baby, called a joey, is born. The newborn is only about 0.8 inches (2 cm) long. It cannot see or hear, and it does not have fur. However, it does have a keen sense of smell.

The joey does not fully leave the mother's body when it is first born. It crawls out from inside her to reach a special pouch she has. It finds its way all on its own using its sense of smell. Once inside the pouch, the joey begins drinking milk from its mother.

During its time in the pouch, the joey grows quickly. After about five months, the joey begins poking its head out of the pouch from time to time to look around. Eventually, it starts climbing all the way out for short periods of time. It returns to the pouch when it wants to rest or hide.

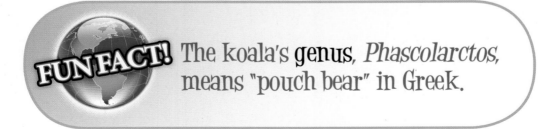

**FUN FACT!** The koala's **genus**, *Phascolarctos*, means "pouch bear" in Greek.

*Newborn koalas are extremely small and fragile.*

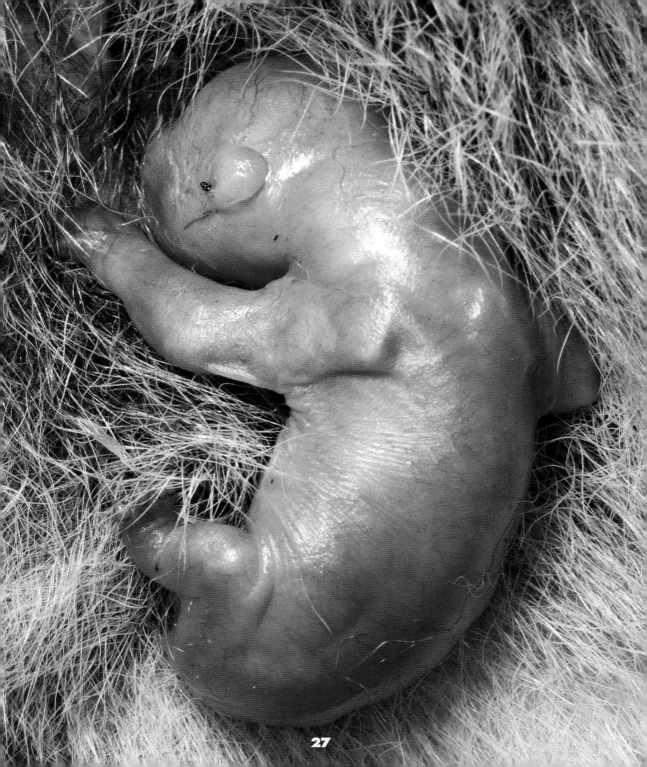

# Growing Up

The joey leaves its mother's pouch for good after about six months. Then it spends all of its time riding on her back or clinging to her belly as she goes about her business. Little by little, the baby learns to eat eucalyptus leaves instead of drinking milk. At first, the mother feeds her joey partially digested leaves that she has chewed up and swallowed. Soon, the joey starts trying to grab at leaves with its mouth as it rides on its mother. This is not very effective, so the joey eventually learns to grip branches and leaves with its paws. During this time, the joey also learns which leaves are the best kind to eat.

Once the joey is about a year old, it is ready to leave its mother. It climbs down to the ground and walks away to find its own **home range**. The young koala continues to grow. It becomes ready to mate and have babies of its own when it is between two and four years old.

*Baby koalas and their mothers are practically inseparable.*

# CHAPTER 4

# Marvelous Marsupials

You may have heard people refer to koalas as "koala bears." At first glance, it is easy to see why someone might think koalas and bears are related. They are both furry, and their bodies have a similar shape. Though they might look alike in some ways, koalas are not bears at all. They are actually a type of animal called a marsupial. Like bears, marsupials are mammals. They are **warm-blooded**, they have hair, and they feed their babies with milk from their bodies. The main thing that sets marsupials apart from other mammals is their pouch.

There are around 250 marsupial species living today. Most of them are found in Australia, New Guinea, and other nearby islands. There are also several dozen marsupial species living in South and Central America. One species lives in North America.

*All marsupials have pouches where their babies can live and grow safely.*

# Ancient Animals

Marsupials have existed for somewhere between 99.6 million and 65.5 million years. Over this time, some marsupial species have changed a great deal. Others disappeared completely. Scientists learn about these ancient animals by studying fossils. Based on where different fossils were found, most experts believe that the first marsupials appeared in South America. From there, marsupials probably traveled to Australia across a connecting strip of land that no longer exists. Once this land disappeared, the marsupials were cut off from other animals. They changed over time to suit their new home. This eventually resulted in the Australian marsupial species we know today.

A koala's early ancestors probably lived very differently than their modern relatives. Instead of climbing up into trees, they likely dug burrows in the ground. This is probably why today's koalas have pouches that open toward their backside. This feature would have kept dirt from getting inside their pouches while they dug.

*Today's koalas lead very different lifestyles from those of their ancestors.*

# Marsupial Cousins

A koala's closest relatives are the other marsupials living in Australia today. Though they have some things in common, there are many differences between these animals. Some are tiny while others are quite large, and diets and lifestyles can vary considerably.

One of the best-known marsupials other than the koala is the kangaroo. There are several different kangaroo species. The red kangaroo is the largest marsupial living today. It can reach heights of almost 7 feet (2 meters). It has extremely strong back legs and feet that it uses to leap across huge distances of Australia's grasslands. Other types of kangaroos are smaller, and some even live in trees like koalas.

Another common Australian marsupial is the wombat, which burrows underground and eats grasses and roots. There is also the marsupial mouse, which looks a lot like a regular mouse. It has a diet of insects and other small animals.

*Like koalas, tree kangaroos are marsupials that spend most of their time climbing through the treetops.*

# CHAPTER 5

# Caring for Koalas

Though koalas face few natural dangers in the wild, there are still many threats to their survival. These issues are all a result of koalas being forced to share their living space with humans. As people build homes, businesses, and other buildings, they clear out eucalyptus forests where koalas live. The koalas are forced to live in smaller and smaller areas. They also have less food to eat.

Roads are another problem. They can separate koalas from one another, making it difficult for the animals to find mates. When koalas try to cross roads, vehicles often hit them. Hundreds of koalas are killed this way each year.

Koalas are often found living in people's backyards or in other areas near humans. Unfortunately, koalas sometimes share such spaces with pet dogs. Dogs will attack koalas that have come down to the ground. These attacks often result in death for the koalas.

*Koalas face great danger anytime they try to cross a busy street.*

# Almost Extinct

There were once several million koalas roaming the wild areas of eastern Australia. Aboriginal Australian people commonly hunted them. But koalas were not killed in excessive numbers, and they were able to thrive. In the early 20th century, however, these incredible animals came close to disappearing forever. People began hunting koalas to collect and sell their fur. The fur was valuable for its use in clothing and other goods. There were no rules about how many koalas could be hunted. As a result, Australia's koala population was reduced to a fraction of its previous size. In some areas where koalas had been common, the animals were almost totally extirpated.

To help save koalas, people brought some of the animals to nearby islands. There, the koalas were able to reproduce without being hunted. As their numbers increased, some of the island koalas were brought back to the mainland. This helped restore some of Australia's damaged koala population.

*A wildlife worker releases a koala back into the wild after it received medical care.*

# Koalas Today

Though koalas are doing better than they were several decades ago, they are still considered a threatened species. There are laws against hunting them, but they still face many other threats. There is very little land set aside for them to live on where they don't have to deal with humans. Experts estimate that there are only between 43,000 and 80,000 koalas living in the wild today. The majority of them make their homes on private property.

If koalas are going to survive long into the future, they will need help from people. Many groups today are working to pass new laws to better protect koalas. Others are working to spread awareness of the dangers of clearing forests where koalas and other animals live. With hard work and greater care, people can help koalas survive amid the many dangers they face today.

*In many areas, there are fewer and fewer trees left for koalas to live in.*

# Words to Know

Aboriginal (ab-uh-RIJ-uh-nuhl) — referring to the native peoples of Australia

ancestors (AN-ses-turz) — ancient animal species that are related to modern species

bacteria (bak-TEER-ee-uh) — microscopic, single-celled living things that exist everywhere and that can either be useful or harmful

burrows (BUR-ohz) — tunnels or holes in the ground made or used as a home by an animal

diet (DYE-it) — the food an animal typically eats

digest (dye-JEST) — to break down food in the organs of digestion so that it can be absorbed into the blood and used by the body

extirpated (EK-stur-pay-tid) — destroyed or removed completely from a specific area

fiber (FYE-bur) — a part of fruits, vegetables, and grains that passes through the body but is not digested

fossils (FOSS-uhlz) — the hardened remains of prehistoric plants and animals

genus (JEE-nuhs) — a group of related plants or animals that is larger than a species but smaller than a family

gland (GLAND) — an organ in the body that produces or releases natural chemicals

habitats (HAB-uh-tats) — places where an animal or a plant is usually found home range (HOME RAYNJ) — area of land in which an animal spends most of its time

mammals (MAM-uhlz) — warm-blooded animals that have hair or fur and usually give birth to live young

mating (MAYT-ing) — joining together to produce babies

nutrients (NOO-tree-ints) — substances such as proteins, minerals, or vitamins that are needed by animals and plants to stay strong and healthy

opposable (uh-POHZ-uh-buhl) — able to be placed against one or more of the remaining fingers or toes of a hand or foot

predators (PRED-uh-turz) — animals that live by hunting other animals for food

solitary (SAH-li-ter-ee) — preferring to live alone

species (SPEE-sheez) — one of the groups into which animals and plants of the same genus are divided

threatened (THRET-uhnd) — at risk of becoming endangered

toxins (TAHK-sinz) — poisonous substances

warm-blooded (WARM-BLUHD-id) — having a warm body temperature that does not change, even if the surrounding temperature is very hot or very cold

# Habitat Map

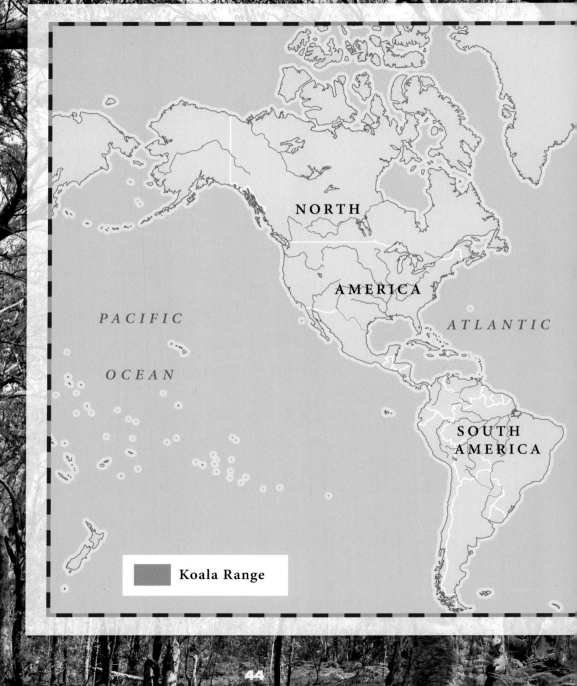

NORTH AMERICA

SOUTH AMERICA

PACIFIC OCEAN

ATLANTIC

Koala Range

ARCTIC OCEAN

EUROPE

ASIA

AFRICA

PACIFIC OCEAN

OCEAN

INDIAN

OCEAN

AUSTRALIA

# Find Out More

**Books**

Bishop, Nic. *Marsupials*. New York: Scholastic, 2009.

Hanel, Rachael. *Koalas*. Mankato, MN: Creative Education, 2009.

Otfinoski, Steven. *Koalas*. Tarrytown, NY: Marshall Cavendish Benchmark, 2008.

Visit this Scholastic Web site for more information on koalas:
**www.factsfornow.scholastic.com**
Enter the keyword **Koalas**

# Index

Page numbers in *italics* indicate a photograph or map.

# About the Author

Josh Gregory is the author of more than 90 books for kids. He has written about everything from animals to technology to history. A graduate of the University of Missouri–Columbia, he currently lives in Portland, Oregon.